Sentences

Howard Nemerov

Sentences

The
University
of Chicago
Press

Chicago and
London

HOWARD NEMEROV, a graduate of Harvard University in 1941,
has taught at a number of colleges and universities and is now
the Edward Mallinckrodt Distinguished University Professor of
English at Washington University in St. Louis. He served as
associate editor of *Furioso* magazine from 1946 to 1951 and was
consultant in poetry to the Library of Congress from 1963 to 1964.
Nemerov has won many notable literary awards, including the
Levinson Prize from *Poetry* magazine, the Fellowship of the
Academy of American Poets in 1971, the 1978 National Book
Award, and the 1978 Pulitzer Prize for Poetry. He was formally
inducted into the American Academy and Institute of Arts
and Letters in 1977. A complete list of his published works
includes:
Verse: *The Image & the Law; Guide to the Ruins; The Salt Garden;
Mirrors & Windows; New and Selected Poems; The Next Room of the
Dream; The Blue Swallows; Gnomes & Occasions; The Western
Approaches; The Collected Poems*
Fiction: *The Melodramatists; Federigo, or the Power of Love; The
Homecoming Game; A Commodity of Dreams & Other Stories;
Stories, Fables & Other Diversitons*
Nonfiction: *Poetry & Fiction: Essays; Journal of the Fictive Life;
Reflections on Poetry & Poetics; Poets on Poetry* (editor)

The University of Chicago Press, Chicago 60637
The University of Chicago Press, Ltd., London

88 87 86 85 84 83 82 81 80   5 4 3 2 1

Library of Congress Cataloging in Publication Data

Nemerov, Howard.
   Sentences.

   I. Title
PS3527.E5S4   811'.54   80–17702
ISBN 0-226-57260-9

for M again, and more than ever now

The author would like to thank the editors of the following journals for permission to reprint poems first appearing in their pages:

The Atlantic Monthly
Alternatives
The Berkeley Poetry Review
Canto
Chicago Review
Chicago Tribune Magazine
Georgia Review
Long Pond Review
Massachusetts Review
Mississippi Review
Mississippi Valley Review
MSS
Nadja (for a limited edition of "By Al Lebowitz's Pool" which first appeared in *The New Republic*)
The New Republic
The New Yorker
Poet and Critic
Poetry: A Magazine of Verse
Rain
River Styx
St. Louis Post-Dispatch
Salmagundi
Subject to Change
Wittenberg Review

"The Unexpected Snow" was first published in a limited edition by the Narwhal Press.

The author wishes also to record his gratitude to Mrs. M. P. Wirthlin for devising and/or discovering the order of the poems.

Contents

1 Beneath

Literature

Is in good hands, it is being written   3
By liberated sex-maniacs, psychologists
With an eye to higher things, and novelists
Convinced they are psychiatric social-workers
With a mission to the slums of the human heart;
It is being written by disgraced politicians
From the safety of minimum-security prisons
With pastel walls affording them protection from
The lower class of criminal while they write
Of finding Jesus, Who has given them
The hundred thousand dollar advance against
The major motion picture soon to be made;
And now new generations of trained chimpanzees
Are manning their machines, moving their lips,
Coming along slowly, all thumbs and unopposable.

The Serial

4   The last year's phone books lying in the rain
With other garbage to be taken away
Are obsolescing programs that contain
The dramatis personae of a play
So vast its purposes and plot
Go ramifying out of mortal sight
In intricate radiations, rise and rot;
Here lie the yellow pages and the white,
Going concerns and bankrupt, where the dead
Hide with the living in the book of life,
The slowly moving serial unread
Whose singles with the husband and the wife
      Are persons parted, who as they leave the stage
      Get quietly stood in for, page by page.

On Growth and Form

Young ones, when your distant grownup kin

At gatherings admire your new height
And say such standard silly things as that
They knew you when you were just so high, or, worse,
When you were just a glint in your father's eye,
Command your high displeasure that it turn
To wonder like the wonder they must feel
And you may feel one day under the roll-
ing wheels of heaven that make up age and time,
At the procrustean miracle of growth
That tripled your length and turned it into height,
And, if you don't take care, may cube your weight,
And being struck with *sagesse* and regret
At having not a verse to bless yourself,
Must mark the moment with a silly say.

6   Police are in there suspecting every book,
An assignment that requires, as I guess,
Great courage and a cheerful skepticism
And the fear of God which is the spring of wisdom.
May teacher and pupil profit from the lesson,
And learn to tremble before they crack a book.

To a Young Scholar Requiring a Reason
He Should Read the Comedy

What may Old Pedant say to you, Young Sir?
"Why, as a *Baedekker* or *Guide Bleu,*
That you mayn't be surprised when you get there."
Though given your newly exhibited character,
The what you say suggesting where you are,
I think that even Alighieri, now,
Whose patient poem deposes case on case
That each of us may know and keep his place,
Might say you needn't read him all that far.

Adoration

When I report at the funerals of friends,
Which happens nowadays oftener than it did,
I am astonished each time over again
At the fucking obsequiousness addressed to God:
O Thou, &c. He's killed this one already,
And is going to do the rest of us
In His own good time, then what in the world
Or out of it's abjection going to get
For either the dead or their smalltime survivors?
Who go to church at ordinary times
To pray to God, who does not go to church.

As for those masses and motets, no matter:
He happens to be tone deaf (or is it stone deaf?
My hearing's not so good either). But once in a way
The music takes me, if it doesn't Him,
The way Bach does the Et In Terra Pax,
Or Mozart does the Tuba Mirum, where
We doomed and damned go on beseeching anyhow.
Does He, when He hears that heavenly stuff, believe?
And at the Lacrimosa does He weep for us?
No end, my friends, to our inventiveness:
God doesn't matter. Adoration does.

Pomp

Angel and urn and broken obelisk
Are but a few of the ideas of the dead
Formed out of legend and the local stone
Set forth in ostentation and all weathers.

Some of the rich have stone doll's houses built,
Apartments where each has his private shelf
Distinct from ditches where the hundreds lie
Tumbled and bulldozed under in one run.

Since all ground's consecrated now, or none,
Our dearly distinguished suicides are here
As well, who took upon themselves to know
The day, the hour, and the means to make an end,

Who quit the world before they could be fired
And at a stroke became to us as gods,
Whose living hands lifted Osiris' veil
And set their sphinx among our pyramids.

Ark

The saving remnant saved, while the rest died?
Let this exception prove my rule of thumb.

Noah's eloquence about the Flood was such
That although mankind didn't heed it much
A couple of fish were so impressed by him
They leapt aboard the Ark and went inside,
Just (as they put it) to be in the swim.

As though to say that grace may simply come,
While works, to work at all, have to be tried.

On the Soul

The prick was the priest that in the first place joined   11
In wedlock the heavy body with the light mind;
The prick stands at the head of every sect;
It is the prick that keeps saying "only connect."
The Dean of St Patrick's had the word, if you'd hear it:
'The thorn in the flesh is become a spur to the spirit.'
The prick is the soul philosophers should have sought:
A kid can get a hard on from pure thought.

New Year's, 1978

12   After the holiday we could finally understand
      Why our eyes come shaped like footballs from God's
         passing hand.

A Male Chauvinist Mermaid

Two troubles with the Equal Rights Amendment: 13
Girls don't get hard ons and boys don't get pregnant.

14   Prig offered Pig the first chance at dessert,
So Pig reached out and speared the bigger part.

"Now that," cried Prig, "is extremely rude of you!"
Pig, with his mouth full, said, "Wha, wha' wou' 'ou do?"

"I would have taken the littler bit," said Prig.
"Stop kvetching, then it's what you've got," said Pig.

      So virtue is its own reward, you see.
      And that is all it's ever going to be.

Riddle with Two Replies

The Ayatollah and the President
Sat down to a common meal; and what ate they?

I used to think it was *Khomeini Grits,*
But now believe it may be *Kurds und Weh.*

War Graves

16   Across the field, above our bulldozed dead,
             Their individual crosses stand parade.

Nixons at Calvary

While the one rides over earth from land to land
Dispensing thunderbolts with even hand,
The other, in the Oval Office all alone,
Is daily mocked, reviled and spat upon.
Which is the suffering servant, which The Boss?
Will the real President Nixon please pick up the Cross?

18

The Secretary spoke of the "facilities."
Under his bald dome the mouth opened and spoke.

The raids, he said, were protection reaction responses
Against the enemy's anti-aircraft facilities

That were harrassing our unarmed reconnaissance
Surveillance over their facilities.

But might the bombs have damaged other targets?
Under his bald dome the mouth opened and spoke.

Possibly, he said, the bombs might have
Deprived the enemy's facilities

Of access to logistic and supply
Facilities in close proximity

To primary targets; by which he meant, I think:
"The bastards kept the bullets near the guns."

Continuous Performances

The war went on till everything was it,
The girls in forage caps, in army coats

From other wars, their skirts dragging in dirt
Where they went parading for world peace now;

Till everyone who was against the war
Was also in it, a tiny nameless part

Of the war, doing what one called "his thing."
Whatever one did, it was something the war could use,

Turning to hand the talents of novelist
And newsboy, shoe clerk and soda jerk—everyone

Had something to contribute all his own
That would nourish the war, the growing war

Already sponsoring movies about itself
To let the children know what it was like.

20   A smile exchanged between a man and a woman
      Across the busy terminal needn't mean
      That they will necessarily fetch up
      Together in a double bed; it merely
      Acknowledges the odds; but all the same,
      Back at the motel in the middle of the night,
      After the Steak Oscar with the King Crab legs
      And the order of french-fried mushrooms on the side
      With the obligatory Sangre di Cristo, pinpoint
      Carbonation blinking at the brink, when he said
      "May we?" and she replied "Mais oui," the two
      Bilingual lovers learning to talk in forked tongues,
      And when she stood there in the middle of the room
      On her round-heeled stilted hi-come-fuck-me shoes,
      "Yes," she breathed, "yes," her eyes jam-packed
          With stars and flowers and titmice.

The Revenants (After a Movie)

Across the barrier of light and shade,
Out of the past that cannot come again,
They come, this crew of revenants
That died in the desert in the shadow of
Their broken aircraft, died and rotted there.
Their shadows rise and speak about their lives
As they would otherwise have been, except . . .
Except. That war, with all its news and noise,
Is gone, its engines and its guns all still,
Its purposes, who knows, achieved or missed,
Merged and submerged in whatever came to pass
Instead, in the history book we have to read
Backward. The barrier of light and shade
Holds, even our illusions have their truth
In the desert where they play; the skeletons
In uniform, the skulls in funny hats.
It was another world they saved, not ours.

Four Soldiers

a sculpture in iron by David Smith

22

Piece by piece recruited from the odd
Detritus of an iron age gone wrong—
Turnbuckle, poker, unidentified
Flanges and bolts—so soldiers get along,
Staggering but yet rigid about the trunk,
One on hands and knees, wounded or else drunk.

Althougth it was an iron discipline
Did this to them, they won their irony
On honorable service; being done
Out of mortality, they are set free
As though by natural virtue in the rust
That answers to their privacy in dust.

Soldier, it is the warfare of the world
Weathers you, and this ruin alone is glory;
Faithfully suffer for the ruining Lord
His timely work, and earn a place in the story.
That way may the machine redeem the part
And nature for some time consent to art.

Coming Home to New York When
It Was Said To Be Going Down the Drain

Descending over The Narrows and across
The great lady carrying her torch for whom,
We flew up river past the bankrupt town
Down to its last Almighty Dollar, turned
On a Hundred and Twenty-Fifth Street, letting down
The wheels and flaps, a pretty tense moment—
Maybe the runways had been repossessed
And towed up Pelham Bay? No, we got down,
And an hour later there we were again
Right in the midst of the biggest damn dream
Everybody ever dreamed at once, Manhattan,
Beautiful recipe for disaster, gone for broke
With half the money of the world in its pocket
And a hole in the pocket, the Port of Entry
And Zone of Interior for the lot of us,
The rejects the retreads the Four-Fs of every last
Country in Europe, our lot that grew up here
And sailed from here to knock the noggins off
Hitler and Mussolini and that mortal god
The Japs adored; and here it is, dead broke,
With lawyers from Albany to Washington
Screaming their parsimonious pieties
Against the wasteful ways of this Great Fact
That in the immortal words of Lazarus

24   Standing out there in the harbor, said
"Give me your garbage, send me whatever can walk,"
And made good every word, and, dying day by day,
Throwing the money away, made ruin renew.

The Three Towns

The road from Adonoi to I Don't Know
Runs on, the elders say, to I Deny.
Whatever won't let us stop won't let us go.

The erected spirit, with its will to know,
Leaves the home town in its own good time to try
The slope from Adonoi to I Don't Know.

The slope so steep, it takes us who knows how
Further from God and closer to the sky;
Whatever won't let us stop won't let us go.

The elders warn, but it is always so:
The beautiful and brash are they that try
The road from Adonoi to I Don't Know

And sometimes in their brilliance mount up so
They finish further on in I Deny;
Whatever won't let us stop won't let us go.

The clear Satanic eminence of How
Runs further to the hermitage of Why.
Whatever won't let us stop won't let us go;
The road from Adonoi? I just don't know.

Conversion

But with minor modifications, gasoline engines can burn pure alcohol—with no pollution of the atmosphere. And by determined national effort, we could replace gasoline from OPEC oil with pure alcohol in our automobiles in the foreseeable future.

—*A Candidate, Soliciting Funds*

What a dream of a scheme! to let the automobile
And not the driver run on bourbonol;
The pump become the instant bar & grille
Getting the country tanked up for the long haul.

By transsubstantiated alcoholine,
Our thinkers say, pollution will be routed,
Travel refined, crude booze will burn us clean,
And only Cadillacs will get polluted.

But it's the pure young men that man the pumps
We worry most about; exposed to sin
At every sale, and like to fall down drumps
With every imperial quart they must put in.

Rush hour traffic too will be a thing to see,
As each consumer in his car consumes
The hootch under the hood, affirming that we
Live not by fuel alone, but by the fumes.

Envoi

Grey candidate, good conscript father and teacher,
We no longer believe in the Unicorn, for Nature
Could never consent to make so odd a creature
(If rhino and narwhal exhibit the unique feature,
They only show how close you've got to watch Her);
But we sure are high on the Foreseeable Future.

Big Red '79

for Mr Wilkinson

28

Life ought to be an imitation of life,
And is. What's said about it is also in it,
Games not excepted. What a season if . . .
A point, and three, and four, in the last minute.

After the death of Cain, not much went right
Except for the ancient tragic recipe
Dictating the good must carry on despite
Misfortune and the odds that they will be

By the better bested, worsted by the worse,
On any afternoon when either lot
Might beat the other lot—only, of course,
Eleven over five it happened not.

A bad time, and a season gone to hell
Now over, and you've been booted out as well
By a wealthy sportsman whose right to raise his voice
No one disputes, and who may well rejoice,

In the ecology of the NFL,
At an easier schedule and a good draft choice.

And still, at the darkening of a sorry year,
Dear sir, I wish the town had kept you here.

An Ace of Hearts

My darling, all these sentiments and signs   29
Of love, what difference posting through the town
The purple hearts, the bloody valentines,
If all are only asses upside down?

30   Ah, Classy Glossy, slick of paper as of prose,
        Where taste is pulled on us like rank by those, God
            knows,
        That know, where liberal views are held up either side
        By ads for youth and beauty, fashion, wealth, and pride:
        An avenue of demonstrators and police
        Contained between tall buildings where the money is.

2 Above

In Zeno's World

Intent upon the target eye
The arrow pierced a garden air
Fragrant with flowers yellow and blue,
It flew beside a shining hedge
And over cobwebs jeweled with dew,
It passed above a still black pool
With a fountain for a heart
Lifting its silver droplets up
So slowly (and the flight so swift)
They stood in air before they fell
Tap tap upon the dark dripstone.
Always, while burrowing in the brain,
Always, and while the victim fell,
The hastening arrow held that still
Moment along its shining shaft.
Its feathers whistled that still air.

Drift

34   A drive diminishing, a sigh between lift
       And sift, it goes along with life, it goes
       Downwind, downstream, you've seen the autumn leaves
       Heap up, the sand and snow seen build their high
       Shouldered escarpments by the grain and flake,
       Assembling the atoms into forms and then
       Dispersing them again, there's nothing wrong
       With drift except as it is said of man,
       Who is not supposed to be a drifter, why
       Not? when it's not by any means a means
       Of doing nothing, but of doing what it does
       Leisurely, easily, with immeasurable
       Deliberation and a grand consent
       Relating to the Tao, which, it is said,
       "Does nothing, yet there's nothing that is not done,"
       Moving across the world meaning to mean
       Something, as if it said, You get my drift?

Monet

Unable to get into the Monet show,
Too many people there, too many cars,
We spent the Sunday morning at Bowl Pond
A mile from the Museum, where no one was,
And walked an hour or so around the rim
Beside five acres of flowering waterlilies
Lifting three feet above their floating pads
Huge yellow flowers heavy on bending stems
In various phases of array and disarray
Of petals packed, unfolded, opening to show
The meaty orange centers that become,
When the ruined flags fall away, green shower heads
Spilling their wealth of seed at summer's end
Into the filthy water among small fish
Mud-colored and duck moving explorative
Through jungle pathways opened among the fronds
Upon whose surface water drops behave
Like mercury, collecting in heavy silver coins
Instead of bubbles; some few redwinged blackbirds
Whistling above all this once in a while,
The silence else unbroken all about.

Acorn, Yom Kippur

36

Look at this little fallen thing, it's got
Its yarmulka still on, and a jaunty sprig
Of a twig, a feather in its cap, and in its head
There is a single-minded thought: *White Oak*.

Language and thought have changed since I was young
And we used to say it had an oak inside,
The way some tribes believe that every man
Has a homunculus inside his head.
Already, though, matter was going out
And energy coming in; though energy
Wasn't the last word either, the last word
Is information, or, more tersely, The Word.
Inside its dreaming head the acorn has
Complete instructions for making an oak
Out of the sun and the local water and soil,
Not to forget the great stretches of time
Required for cracking the code, solving the script,
Translating the sacred book of the white oak
With its thousands of annual leaves and their footnotes
—Amounting to millions in a century—
Instructing the oak in the making of acorns
And so forth and so on, world without end.

What the moral of this may be I do not know.
But once a mystical lady in a dream

Beheld her Savior, an acorn in his hand,
And asking what might this be was answered thus:
"It is in a manner everything that is made."

Insomnia I

Some nights it's bound to be your best way out,
When nightmare is the short end of the stick,
When sleep is a part of town where it's not safe
To walk at night, when waking is the only way
You have of distancing your wretched dead,
A growing crowd, and escaping out of their
Time into yours for another little while;

Then pass ghostly, a planet in the house
Never observed, among the sleeping rooms
Where children dream themselves, and thence go down
Into the empty domain where daylight reigned;
Reward yourself with drink and a book to read,
A mystery, for its elusive gift
Of reassurance against the hour of death.
Order your heart about: *Stop doing that!*
And get the world to be secular again.

Then, when you know who done it, turn out the light,
And quietly in darkness, in moonlight, or snowlight
Reflective, listen to the whistling earth
In its backspin trajectory around the sun
That makes the planets sometimes retrograde
And brings the cold forgiveness of the dawn
Whose light extinguishes all stars but one.

Insomnia II

He watching over Israel
  Slumbers not nor sleeps

To whom else, God, but thee shall I complain?
Should I be grateful that you made me me
And not another? For the selfsame pain
Would then attend me that attends me now,
The pain of self dear to itself and vain
Of being self, and fearful of the loss of self
In death, or an eternity of pain
Suffered in self not capable to die
And rid itself of self, against the grain
To thirst after oblivion and be
Time after time denied? That would profane
Even a human mercy, and how much more thine;
Or wouldst thou, still worse, make me live again?

And then I think the world a sea of pain
Whose every wave is born a human soul
Able to hurt to the very sake of pain,
And that the centuries of this that pass
Are but a moment in your watch over this pain,
Unsleeping god, self-doomed to see our pain,
Would God that I could sing thee asleep again.

First Things, and Last

40   So brief, so brave, so april pale
The little flowering before the leaves
Unfold themselves, the crocus opening amidst
The melting snow, the blue grape hyacinth,
Chalice of tulip swayed on slender stem—
Forsythia's yellow, watercolor-wet;
And sudden the sun's first warmth upon your face—

It makes us weep a bit for gratitude,
Poor foolish creatures we were doomed to be,
Born, as Augustine saith, twixt stale and stool.

There will be flowers at our funerals,
Pale flowers of spring, and, for an epitaph,
"They had a touch of class. But just a touch."

Morning Glory

Convolvulus it's called as well, or ill,
And bindweed, though sweating gardeners
Believe it rightly christened The Devil's Guts.

After it's tied whole hedges up in knots
And strangled all the flowers in a bed
And started to ambition after trees,

It opens out its own pale trumpet-belled
Five-bladed blooms—from white of innocence
Shading to heavenly blue—so frail they fall
At almost a touch, and even left alone
      Endure but a day.

During a Solar Eclipse

42   The darkening disk of the moon before the sun
        All morning moves, turning our common day
        A deep and iris blue, daylight of dream
        In which we stand bemused and looking on
        Backward at shadow and reflected light,

        While the two great wanderers among the worlds
        Enter their transit with our third, a thing
        So rare that in his time upon the earth
        A man may see, as I have done, but four,
        In childhood two, a third in youth, and this

        In likelihood my last. We stand bemused
        While grass and rock darken, and stillness grows,
        Until the sun and moon slide out of phase
        And light returns us to the common life
        That is so long to do and so soon done.

The Dying Garden

The flowers get a darkening brilliance now,
And in the still sun-heated air stand out
As stars and soloists where they had been before
Choruses and choirs; at the equinox,
I mean, when the great gyroscope begins
To spin the sun under the line and do
Harvest together with fall: the time that trees
Crimp in their steepled shapes, the hand of leaf
Become a claw; when wealth and death are one,
When moth and wasp and mouse come in the house
For comfort if they can; the deepening time
When sketchy Orion begins his slow cartwheel
About the southern sky, the time of turn
When moth and wasp and mouse come in the house
To die there as they may; and there will be,
You know, All Saints, All Souls, and Halloween,
The killing frost, the end of Daylight Time,
Sudden the nightfall on the afternoon
And on children scuffling home through drifts of leaf;
Till you drop the pumpkins on the compost heap,
The blackened jack o'lanterns with their candled eyes,
And in the darkening garden turn for home
Through summer's flowers now all gone, withdrawn,
The four o'clocks, the phlox, the hollyhocks,
Somber November in amber and umber embering out.

Negative Proof

1

However did people get to know
That no two snowflakes are alike?
I have never heard this law disputed
Or even challenged, nor do I know
The evidence for it or for
The tone of assuming certainty
In which it is always said. Right now
Outside my window there must be
As many snowflakes as there are
Protozoa in the Atlantic Ocean
Or atoms in the Encyclopedia,
But these people with their insolence
Go right on putting it about
That no two snowflakes are alike.
Perhaps it is a point of faith,
One of these never-questioned items
Beneath even the level of assumption,
On which civilisations are said to rest.

Notice that no one ever writes:
"I personally have never seen
Two snowflakes that were just alike,"
Which would be humble if unremarkable
Except as a feat of memory.

No, the statement always takes
The form of law, and if you ask
About it, people look surprised
And a little piqued before they say:
"It is a scientific fact."

2

In a dream I found two snowflakes just alike,
The spit and mirror each of other, spike
To his spike. I put them in the refrigerator,
Determined to get up a little later
And check my facts. But though I overslept
Next morning I discovered they had kept.

In much excitement I sat down to write
The revelation granted in the night,
The cold, dispassionate account that will,
If I am not mistaken, help fill
Certain lacunae in the present state
Of physical knowledge, as well as make me great
Among the learned, with a secure fame,
A fellowship, and an immortal name
Whose influence will continue to be felt
When my dream's forgotten, and my snowflakes melt.

A Christmas Storm

46   All Sunday and Sunday night, cold water drops
At the will of heaven, freezing where it hits,
Glazing the windshields and the glistening ways,
Sheathing the branches and the power lines
In leaden insulations uniform
Across the counties and the towns, until
Connections loosen out and lines come down
And limbs that had sustained the horizontal
A hundred years unstrained crack under the weight
Of stiffened wet and short transformers out
So that ten thousand homes turned suddenly off
Go grey and silent, and the cold comes in
Slowly at first, then faster, drifting through
The window frames ghostly, under doors,
While night comes on and provident families
Remember where the candles and lanterns were
From last year, and other families don't;
While lucky families light fires, and others can't
But bundle up in blankets or skid downstreet
To the kindness of their neighbors or their kin,
And cars caught out are paralyzed at hills,
And it is clear that the relentless rain
Will go unrelentingly on till it relents:

Which it does do only next day at dawn,
When sunrise summons up the pride of the eye

To radiant brocades of fabergé'd

Drainpipes and eaves and scintillant fans
Of bush and tree turned emblems of themselves;
Where every twig is one and three, itself,
Its chrysalis in ice transparent, and last
Haloed in splintering light, as in the great
Museum of mind the million Christmas trees
Illuminate their diamonded display
To crystalline magnificent candelabra
Of silver winking ruby and emerald and gold
As angled to the sun by the glittering wind,
To show forth, to show up, to show off
The rarely tinselled treasures of the world
Before the powerful, before the poor.

The Unexpected Snow

48
The networks knew nothing of it, or if they did
It was two states west of us and heading south,

But as February's light began to fade
The flakes began to fall, speckles at first

But growing fast till they reminded us
Of moths clustered about the cold street light,

A mortal permanence fluttering all ways
At once yet averaging out to gravity

So that by morning half a foot of it,
Allowing an inch or so each way for drift,

Had lifted the level of the winter ground
Unpromising and brown, and made it white

With shadows blue under the blue spruce
And melting masses collapsing off the roof

In small catastrophes that never harmed
So much as a cat; and all this came about

On a Friday night, leaving us two clear days
Not having to drive, not having to get somewhere,

Comfortable in the warm house with radio
And TV, records and books, even with thoughts

About the cold and murderous world, and how
We managed in it for a little while.

Easter

50   Even this suburb has overcome Death.
        Overnight, by a slow explosion, or
        A rapid burning, it begins again
        Bravely disturbing the brown ground
        With grass and even more elaborate
        Unnecessaries such as daffodils
        And tulips, till the whole sordid block
        Of houses turned so inward on themselves,
        So keeping of a winter's secret sleep,
        Looks like a lady's hat, improbably
        Nodding with life, with bluejays hooting
        And pigeons caracoling up among
        The serious chimney pots, and pairs
        Of small birds speeding behind the hedges
        Readying to conceal them soon. Here,
        Even here, Death has been vanquished again,
        What was a bramble of green barbed wire
        Becomes forsythia, as the long war
        Begins again, not by our doing or desiring.

Ceremony

At five of this winter morn the hound and I
Go out the kitchen door to piss in the snow,
As we have done in all solemnity
Since he was a pup and would wake me up to go.

We mingle our yellow waters with the white
In a spatter of silence under the wheeling skies
Wherein the failing moon lets fall her light
Between Orion and the Pleiades.

Hyperbole (I)

On the ground he's only the twitch of a nose,
The switch of a tail, and a tremor in between;
The Woody Allen of the animals,
Epitome of the at-all-times-terrified life.

Come near his tree, he gets 'round the other side
At the speed of a shadow hiding from the sun;
And he digs so many Swiss numbered accounts
He can't remember where he hid the nuts.

But going aloft he's got Olympic poise:
The flow of fur along the outer limb,
The synapse-crossing leap from tree to tree;

Maybe above all the death-defying act
On the high wire, quick as a telegram
Whatever the message never losing its cool.

Hyperbole (II)

Fat flying rats freighted with fleas and puffed
To pouting with importance on the ground,
Necks ruffed with a dirty iridescence that
Ambitions toward the rainbow but fetches up
Resembling some kind of Victorian hairball,
Their tiny pea-heads incessantly pecking away
At even the speckled, unrewarding walk,
They look the way the poets sound,
Splendid in flight and stupid on the ground;
But when they rise and go, in flights arrayed
And squadrons that cross and change and yet remain
A flowing constant, it's into beauty, and
The eye bemused must follow them away
Evanescing in distances of cloudless blue.

Innocence

54   Hours long last night
The storm stood over me
Swinging the bright blade of its light
Repeatedly about my rooftree
While the rain came down
  So hard it bounced.

This morning, innocence again.
Thin water on the graveled ground
Rippled the light reflectively
Of a pale blue and cloud-strewn sky
That didn't know what it had done,
  And no more did I.

A Catch

Throwing alone wouldn't be fun,
And catching alone can't be done.
The two of them together, though,
      Are among the very few
      Things human beings do
That make us look as if we know
A world, and are at home in it,
Where lock and key exactly fit.

To watch the throwing of a ball,
Its free rise, necessary fall,
To see the link across the sky
      Develop from one hand
      And meet the other hand,
The claim completed by the sigh—
It is to know the beautiful
As barely halfway natural.

Nor do I mean just the expert,
The long pass or the throw from third,
Lovely as those things are; I mean
      A catch between anyone,
      A father & a son,
Makes visible something unseen,
How from the father's hand is hurled
To be held the hard ball of the world.

Walking the Dog

Two universes mosey down the street
Connected by love and a leash and nothing else.
Mostly I look at lamplight through the leaves
While he mooches along with tail up and snout down,
Getting a secret knowledge through the nose
Almost entirely hidden from my sight.

We stand while he's enraptured by a bush
Till I can't stand our standing any more
And haul him off; for our relationship
Is patience balancing to this side tug
And that side drag; a pair of symbionts
Contented not to think each other's thoughts.

What else we have in common's what he taught,
Our interest in shit. We know its every state
From steaming fresh through stink to nature's way
Of sluicing it downstreet dissolved in rain
Or drying it to dust that blows away.
We move along the street inspecting it.

His sense of it is keener far than mine,

And only when he finds the place precise
He signifies by sniffing urgently
And circles thrice about, and squats, and shits,
Whereon we both with dignity walk home
And just to show who's master I write the poem.

The Little Aircraft

58   The little aircraft trudging through night, cloud, rain,
Is neither alone nor lost amid the great
Inverted ocean of the air, for a lane
Invisible gives it intelligence,
The crossing needles keep its heading right,
The neutrally numbering voices of its friends
Make of its blindness blind obedience,
From one to another handing its destiny on
The stages of the way with course and height
Till finally it's funneled in and down
Over the beacons along the narrowing beam,
Perfectly trusting a wisdom not its own,
That breaking out of cloud it may be come
Back to this world and to be born again,
Into the valley of the flarepath, fallen home.

Achievement

Some seven miles above the Middle West
With Denver and the Rockies being dragged
Beneath our notice at the speed of sound
Nearly if not quite making the sun stand still
With drink in hand and dinner soon to come
And plastic stethoscope stuck in the ears
Hearing an orchestra in Düsseldorf
Obedient to the instructions of a dead
Musician a couple of hundred years away
Putting his symphony in parenthesis
Inside a bored and inattentive skull
Lifted aloft on four barrels of flame
Farting their way across the continent,
This sentence in an airline magazine:
"We do not understand the human brain."

The Print-out

60 at first light
this very day
a pick-up flight,
starling and grackle,
blackbird and may-
be the odd jay,
a motley lot
that'd heard the word
though not of mouth,
was heading south—

transmitting it
by bit and bit
of one design:
wings shut/minus
wings spread/plus,
the no, the yes,
saying what they
were meant to say

that out of those
implicit clues
we might suppose
that there are some
for whom
what everyone knows
is noise
is news

The Plain Fact

62   The plain fact of the matter's that I saw
A turkey buzzard circling low above
The Old Folks' Home on Trinity behind
The Synagogue. A sight can't get much more
Explicit than that, and in a poem it'd be
A recipe for getting disbelieved;
Which didn't stop the bird from being there,
The people on the porch from looking up
And thinking silently of God knows what,
Nor me, the passing scribe, from putting down
The plain and fancy fact wherever found:
The sirens singing on the boulevard
A block away, answering to the crime,
The accident, the seizure in the street;
What matter where the buzzard makes his rounds?

3 *Beyond*

The Makers

Who can remember back to the first poets,
The greatest ones, greater even than Orpheus?
No one has remembered that far back
Or now considers, among the artifacts
And bones and cantilevered inference
The past is made of, those first and greatest poets,
So lofty and disdainful of renown
They left us not a name to know them by.

They were the ones that in whatever tongue
Worded the world, that were the first to say
Star, water, stone, that said the visible
And made it bring invisibles to view
In wind and time and change, and in the mind
Itself that minded the hitherto idiot world
And spoke the speechless world and sang the towers
Of the city into the astonished sky.

They were the first great listeners, attuned
To interval, relationship, and scale,
The first to say above, beneath, beyond,
Conjurors with love, death, sleep, with bread and wine,
Who having uttered vanished from the world
Leaving no memory but the marvelous
Magical elements, the breathing shapes
And stops of breath we build our Babels of.

By Al Lebowitz's Pool

1

Imagine this: three beach balloons of three
Sizes, sometimes spinning and sometimes not,
Float in the transparent water table
Reflecting light blue light up from the floor.
They slightly sink into their own images
Mirrored below themselves as bubbles a bit
Elongate gaining and losing their various colors
According as they move between sun and shade,
Shade of the sailing cloud, shade of the oak
And sycamore and apple standing over
Or bending above, and through the dappled light
Respondingly they drift before light airs,
Sailing in independence that is yet
Relation, unpredictable if not
Quite free, mysteriously going about
Their balancing buoyancies sometimes puffed
On some bits of V-shaped wake; like a mobile
By Calder, only more so—linkages
Invisible, of wind and the watching mind,
Connect and vary their free-hand forms. The world
Is a misery, as it always was; these globes
Of color bob about, a mystery
Of pure relation that looks always right

Whatever it does. A steel-blue-black wasp
Rides on one ball awhile, flies to the next,
Possibly playing, possibly not; by law
Any three things in the wide world
Triangulate: the wasp, and Betelgeuse,
And Our Lady of Liberty in the harbor; if
It's any comfort to us, and it is.

2

Sunshine and rain at once, and the clear pool
At once lights up its light and shadow show,
Doing its free-hand random perfect circles
That on a nucleus of bubble and drop
Grow outward and silently intersect
Without collision or consequence, as if
They lived between the spirit and the world,
And evanescing are replaced by others
In patterns that repeat themselves beneath
In light and shade that seem to ripple away
Between the surface and the floor and dazzle
Again against the sunshine side. Dame Kind
Is doing one of her mighty and meaningless
Experimental demonstrations, but

Of What? Playing, perhaps, with the happiness of
A couple of groups of aperiodic crystals
Like thee and me, who are old enough to know
That if these moments could not pass away
They could not be, all dapple and delight.

3

Two girls in the pool, two old men out of it
Observing with an implicit kind of love
Mildly distinguished from lechery, much from lust,
The slender strong young bodies sudden as fish
To dive and swerve in the dazzled element
And surface (no longer much like fish at all)
Smiling, their long hair asparkle as with stars.
The old men, relaxed into their middle ages
And comfortable in the flesh for yet awhile,
Whom generation has had its will and fill of
And nearly if not quite let go, smile back
Over their drinks and banter with the girls
In a style that allows courtship and courtesy
To show their likenesses and keep their distance,
Just glancingly at risk; and the young women
Kindly respond in kind. No one, praise God,

Is going to get in trouble this time around.
It is late Sunday morning by the pool,
A Sunday morning late in summer time,
A Sunday morning of the middle class,
And no one, praise God, is even like to drown
Before it's time to go indoors for lunch.

4

Likely the last of the summer's storms goes by,
And even the water in the pool looks lank,
With leaves already dead upon its flat
Spinning a while and sinking waterlogged,
A couple of struggling bugs doing the same.
Even the heat begins to ember out,
The year has perceptibly started down again,
And summer's wondering stillness is on the move
Over ourselves as well; a leaf comes down
And alights without a splash; another year
Of the little lot has passed, and what have we
Squirreled away more than this summer's day
With the electric storm hammering down on it
Releasing life? The banked furnace of the sun
With reliquary heat returns in splendor

Diminished some with time, but splendid still.
Beside the pool we drink, talk, and are still,
These times of kindness mortality allows.

5

An afternoon alone beside the pool
Observing, or more like peaceably taking in,
Recording, stillness made of rippling wave
And waving leaf, of shadow and reflected light,
And silence able to draw into its dream
The siren singing on the avenue,
The crying of a child two houses down,
The aircraft laboring through four thousand feet
On the way elsewhere. Stillness and silence still,
Shimmering frequencies of waterlight
Reflected from the planes of leaf above
And from the screening panels of the pool,
So many white oscilloscopes whereon
The brimming water translates into light.

Reflection and reflexion, lovely words
I shall be sorry to let go when I let go:
Reflected light, reflexion of the wave;

For things reflected are more solemn and still
Than in themselves they are, it is the doubling
Perhaps that seems to bring them nearer thought;
Could we reflect, did water not reflect?

Enchanted afternoon, immune from time,
Illusion's privilege gives me the idea that I
Am not so much writing this verse as reading it
Up out of water and light and shadow and leaf
Doing the dance of their various dependencies—
As if I might daydream my way again
Into the world and be at one with it—
While the shadows of harder, more unyielding things
Edge steadily and stealthily around the pool
To translate the revolving of the world
About itself, the spinning ambit of the seasons
In the simple if adamant equation of time
Around the analemma of the sun.

Remembering Ford Madox Ford and Parade's End

for Sondra Stang

Beginning with two young men before The War,
Young men 'of the English public official class'
'In the perfectly appointed railway carriage'—
Lord Russell would say, a couple of worlds away
As usual, that he pitied his children
Because nobody born since Nineteen-Twelve
Could have known a moment's happiness; nobody,
He should have said, of the middle class and up,
Like your two young men, Macmaster starting out
On the social and sexual climb and Tietjens
The yeoman at statistics and sufferings—
Beginning your four gospels about a world
Threatened by nothing more than suffragettes,
As outward and as *there* as it had been
For Jane and George but showing its omens forth
In clerical madness, fog, and a fatal smash
Between the automobile and the horse;
Progressing as it had to do into mud and death
With but one memory of Bemerton's parish priest:—
     Sweet day, so cool, so calm, so bright,
     The bridall of the earth and skie—
And back to London in hysterical victory,
The adjutant's cry across the square: "There will be
No more parades;" and thence to England's remains,
The winding down in one poor dying mind

Not even the hero's, the great house sold away
And the great tree cut down—dear God, dear Ford,
It's like that earlier English myth of how
Before the Tudors it was all roast beef
And wassail ale and the Yule log and the boar's head
In hand bear I; yet we, who did the next
Big one entailed upon us at Versailles,
Read you and believe your word. They were,
As we are, a sorry lot; you made them good.

The Historical Judas

74   He too has an eternal part to play,
     What did he understand? that good has scope
     Only from evil, flowering in filth?
     Did he go smiling, kissing, to betray
     Out of a fine conviction of his truth,
     Or some original wreckage of our hope?

     If merely mistaken, at any rate,
     He had a talent for the grand mistake,
     The necessary one, without which not,
     And managed to incur eternal hate
     For triggering what destiny had got
     Arranged from the beginning, for our sake.

     Let us consider, then, if not forgive
     This most distinguished of our fellow sinners,
     Who sponsored our redemption with his sin,
     And whose name, more than ours, shall surely live
     To make our meanness look like justice in
     All histories commissioned by the winners.

A Myth among the Clerisy

The intellectuals have an esoteric myth
Which is hardly heard of, and never believed,
Outside of universities, and that is why
It is such a splendid myth. It goes like this:

Somewhere back in the sacramental high sublime,
Between Aquinas, say, and Alighieri, all was wonderful.
Alighieri seems not to have noticed this, but it is thought
He stood too close to his canvas to get the big picture.
Anyhow, wonderful. A primal, paradisal unity
Of thoughts and things. The world might have been
   made by God.

But then we sinned and fell. We sinned and fell
With Abelard, with Scotus, and with Occam; sinned and
   fell
With Roger Bacon and Sir Francis Bacon; sinned and fell
With Descartes and Newton and Leibniz and Locke; we
   sinned and fell
Into nominalism, thence into skepticism, thence into
   materialism,
Empiricism, positivism, behaviorism, Marxism,
   Freudianism,
And a pandemonium of other isms, including
   scientism—

Meanwhile, we were hit, and right in the same decade, too,
With The Origin of Species and the Second
  Thermodynamical Law,
Which got us hung up between evolutionism and
  degradationism,
Between vitalism and mechanism, followed by a host of
  other isms
Followed in turn by war and the various ends of the
  world.

All this we richly deserved to have happen, and it did.

But now, by the discovery of uncertainty relations,
The development of statistical ideas of cause,
And the paradoxical behavior of single electrons
Confronted by a choice between two holes,
Mystery has been restored to the universe.
And when all this is fully understanded of the people,
God will become more sympathetic to mankind,
The real estate developer will run on charity,
And the blade of the bulldozer bite not so keen.

So runs the myth among the clerisy.
If any among you believe it, let him be
Deported to the thirteenth century, preferably in
  December.

Museum

The trees that mass-produce their leaves each spring
Offend the conoisseur, the sensitive
Handmaiden type who is in love with art;
Here is the one-of-a-kindness of everything,

Climate-controlled against weathering time,
Bought with the money, warranted by wealth,
Gone on the public, but with reverence;
Here must be where the gods go when they die—

The naked ladies and the red-clad cardinals,
The young man dead across the young girl's knees,
Landscapes receding as salvation does
Into a clear and vision-finishing blue;

The plain geometries of the face of truth,
Perspective lines obedient vanishing at
The vanishing point, and the beholder's eye
Beholden even at disappointment's end

Where the sacred secret might have been profaned
In a girl's smile or a patch of yellow wall,
But wasn't, as the picture-plane maintained
A distant stillness; very god displayed
Like a banjo crosswise on his mother's knees.

At an Exhibition of Muslim Calligraphy

78   Forbidden from making images, they wrote
       Their sacred graffiti on every surface and
       In all materials to hand, satin to silver,
       Stone, steel, silk, so that their household things
       Doubled as prayers. Now all this gorgeous stuff,
       Collected far from home and far downstream
       Has been by money's magic changed in kind:
       Now it is Art, enclosed in glass, dramatically
       Poised, and illuminated by spotlights set
       In the ceiling high above, leaving the rest
       Of the rooms in cathedral gloom, so that
       We go with a kind of reverence after all,
       Softly, and not speaking above a whisper,
       Reading ourselves the explanatory cards
       Like invitations placed beside each piece
       And looking dumbly at scimitars inscribed
       With Allah's name, at jewel boxes and
       Cosmetics caskets inscribed with Allah's name.
       It is a strange experience, this of *Art:*
       We wander among writings, understanding not a word.

Thanksgrieving

Infant mortality didn't, as they say, claim me
(though it damn near did), so I grew what they call up.
To the childhood illnesses routine for those times
I added only para-typhoid on my own.
Was never starved, nor did my parents
Whip me or leave me chained to the bed;
Nor did I get born, a Jew, in Germany,
Plus I went to their war and didn't die of it.
Leaving aside my adventures among the dentists—
"Your teeth are fine, but those gums have got to go"—
My skirmishes with medicine include
But a couple of major operations and a few
Discomfortable bothers with skeleton and strings.
Have so far stayed out of asylums and jails,
And given the smallth and fewth of my abilities
Have been lucky in being steadily employed.
Am still with the same dame, have three sons,
Have lost to death up to this day only a few
Immediate family and five good friends—

So help me, life, I may still make it to the end.

The Author to His Body
on Their Fifteenth Birthday, 29 ii 80

"There's never a dull moment in the human body."
—*The Insight Lady*

80

Dear old equivocal and closest friend,
Grand Vizier to a weak bewildered king,
Now we approach The Ecclesiastean Age
Where the heart is like to go off inside your chest
Like a party favor, or the brain blow a fuse
And the comic-book light-bulb of Idea black out
Forever, the idiot balloon of speech
Go blank, and we shall know, if it be knowing,
The world as it was before language once again;

Mighty Fortress, maybe already mined
And readying to blow up grievances
About the lifetime of your servitude,
The body of this death one talkative saint
Wanted to be delivered of (not yet!),
Aggressively asserting your ancient right
To our humiliation by the bowel
Or the rough justice of the elderly lecher's
Retiring from this incontinence to that;

Dark horse, it's you we've put the money on
Regardless, the parody and satire and
The nevertheless forgiveness of the soul
Or mind, self, spirit, will or whatever else
The ever-unknowable unknown is calling itself

This time around—shall we renew our vows?
How should we know by now how we might do
Divorced? Homely animal, in sickness and health,
For the duration; buddy, you know the drill.

To His Piano

82   Old friend, patient of error as of accuracy,
Ready to think the fingerings of thought,
You but a scant year older than I am
With my expectant mother expecting maybe
An infant prodigy among her stars
But getting only little me instead—

To see you standing there for six decades
Containing Chopsticks, Für Elise, and
The Art of Fugue in your burnished rosewood box,
As well as all those years of silence and
The stumbling beginnings the children made,
Who would believe the twenty tons of stress
Your gilded frame's kept stretched out all this while?

Elegy

My Thompson, least attractive character
Among the four because so fierce of character,
Whiny and scrawny, rolling on the floor
To be caressed, and scratching when you were,

There'll be three dishes now instead of four
Morning and night, and three to be let out the door
And in the door, and only you no more
Scratching the glass to be let in before,

All that about nine lives a lie, or else
One of the cruel deceits of fairy tales,
All nine bestowed at birth, and all the false
Nine taken at a stroke. Now what avails
Your caterwauling in that sightless See?
If Death should stroke thee, Thompson, scratch Him
    for me.

Instant Replay

84   My dear, this is the first age of the world
        To give us back the world the way it was
        A moment back; immediate proustian *recherche*
        Or slow or still, no longer out of reach
        If still irrevocable; like the plea of Faust,
        The second sight, the drowning life reviewed.

        It will always be exactly the way it was.

Because You Asked about
the Line between Prose and Poetry

Sparrows were feeding in a freezing drizzle   85
That while you watched turned into pieces of snow
Riding a gradient invisible
From silver aslant to random, white, and slow.

There came a moment that you couldn't tell.
And then they clearly flew instead of fell.